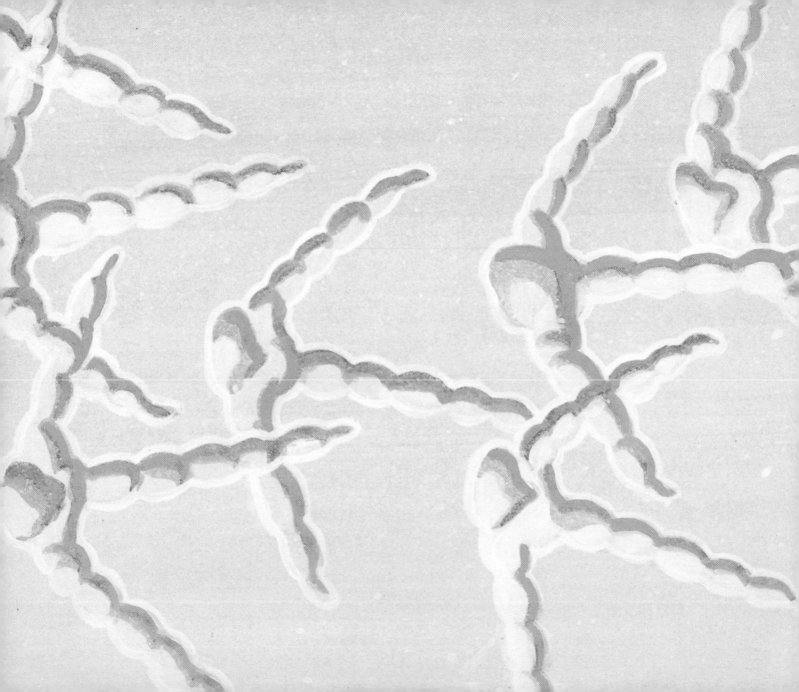

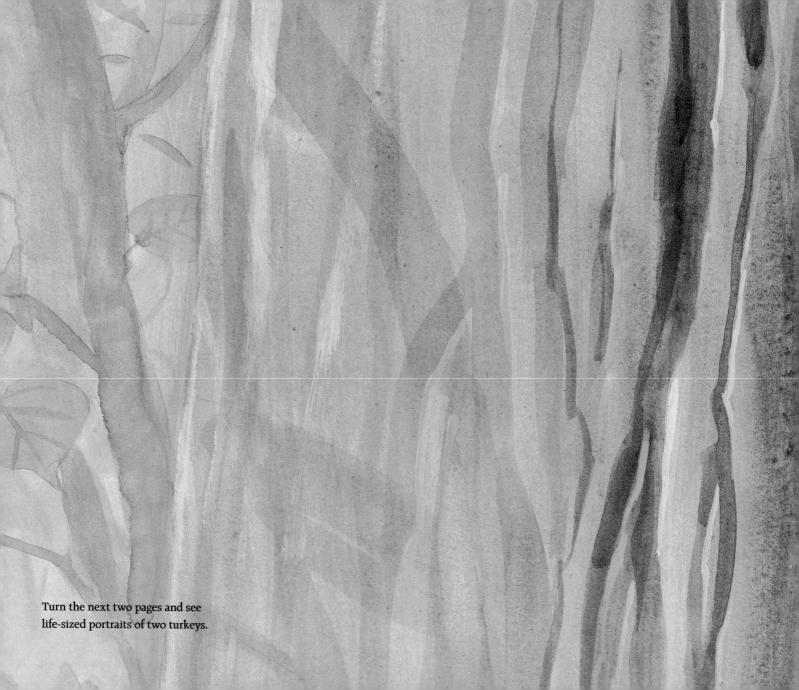

Turn the next two pages and see
life-sized portraits of two turkeys.

Jim Arnosky's
ALL ABOUT Turkeys

SCHOLASTIC

New York Toronto London Auckland Sydney
Mexico City New Delhi Hong Kong Buenos Aires

This book was originally published in hardcover by Scholastic Press in 1998.

ISBN-13: 978-0-590-69780-4
ISBN-10: 0-590-69780-3

12 11 10 9 8 7 6 5 4 3 2 1   8 9 10 11 12 13/0

Printed in the U.S.A.   23
This edition first printing, April 2008

The artwork for this book was created using acrylic paint
in a translucent style on acid-free watercolor paper.

The text type was set in Raleigh.

Book design by Kristina Iulo

For Susan,
who watches wild turkeys
throughout the year

Have you ever wondered
about turkeys?
Where are wild turkeys found
and how do they live?
What do turkeys eat?
Where do they sleep?
How big can a wild turkey grow?

This book answers these questions
about turkeys and more.
It is all about turkeys!

Turkeys are big, strong, hardy birds.
Wild turkeys are very wary. They may
be the most wary of all birds.

Most of the time you see wild turkeys they are away, in the distance. You can only see their dark shapes as they move or feed.

Female turkey

Male turkey

beard

When seen much closer, those dark shapes become iridescent and shine bronze, red, and blue in the sunlight.

Male turkeys, called toms, are larger than female turkeys, which are called hens. The males are more deeply colored than the females, and are more apt to have a beard than the females. Turkey beards grow from the base of the throat and hang straight down.

Turkeys that live in desert regions are more tan in color than woodland turkeys.

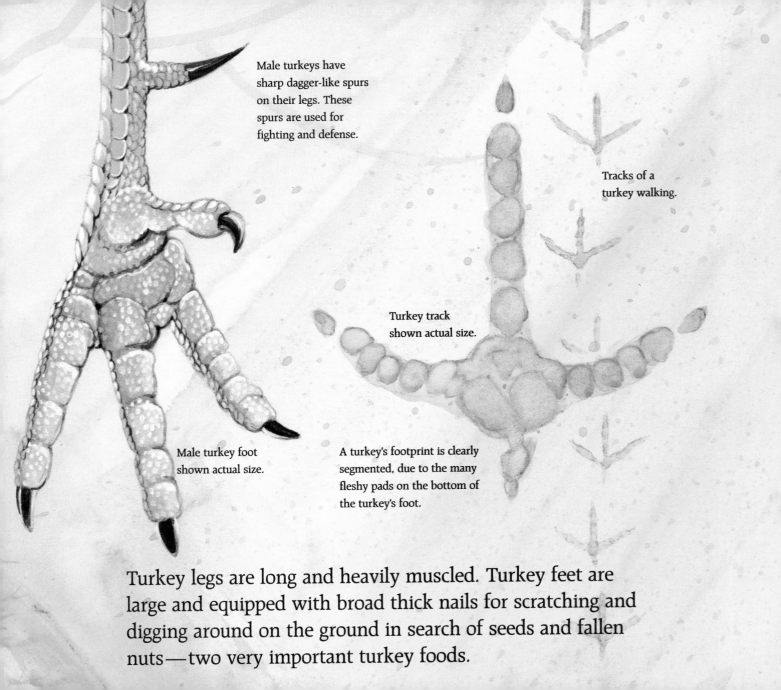

Male turkeys have sharp dagger-like spurs on their legs. These spurs are used for fighting and defense.

Tracks of a turkey walking.

Turkey track shown actual size.

Male turkey foot shown actual size.

A turkey's footprint is clearly segmented, due to the many fleshy pads on the bottom of the turkey's foot.

Turkey legs are long and heavily muscled. Turkey feet are large and equipped with broad thick nails for scratching and digging around on the ground in search of seeds and fallen nuts—two very important turkey foods.

The weird-looking protrusion on a turkey's head is called the caruncle. When a turkey is agitated, its caruncle will extend and hang over the face or beak.

A turkey has no feathers on its head, only a scattering of short hairs. This is what one male turkey's head looked like to me as seen enlarged through my telephoto lens.

Silhouette shows actual size turkey head and neck.

The fleshy folds of skin under a turkey's chin are called the wattles.

The head's ability to change color is most evident and more vibrant in males. A complete change from dull to brilliant can occur in less than a minute.

The two portraits on these pages show the same bird in only a minute's difference.

Each turkey eye has a broad monocular view. Because the eyes can look forward together, a turkey has binocular (3-dimensional) vision as well.

The head and throat of a turkey can change color from an overall gray or violet, when the bird is calm, to tri-colored red, white, and blue. The tri-coloring happens when the turkey is excited or agitated.

How well a turkey can smell is unknown. A turkey's hearing is excellent. Its eyesight, incredible! Turkeys can see the smallest, slightest movement a hundred yards away.

CANADA

The dark colored area shows the turkey's original range, along with places where the birds have been introduced by humans and have become firmly established.

The rest of the colored area shows where turkeys have more recently been introduced and populations are taking hold.

UNITED STATES

MEXICO

Where you see one turkey you most likely will see more. They travel in flocks in part for the protection such numbers of individuals provide, and in part because the best feeding and hiding places draw them together.

Turkeys are animals of edge lands—wherever field meets woods, or brush borders open plain. On these edges they find and eat nuts, seeds, grains, berries, greens, and any insects they can catch. In farm country, turkeys frequent cornfields after harvest when leftover kernels of corn remain scattered over the ground.

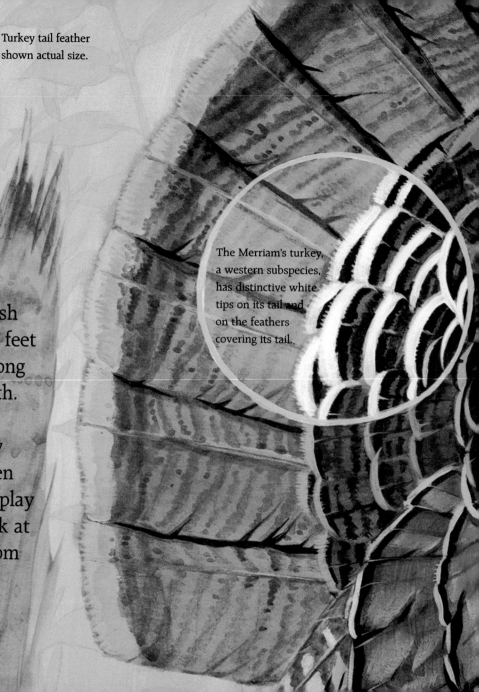

Adult male turkeys are sometimes called gobblers after the loud gobbling sound they make when proclaiming their dominance. Two gobblers claiming the same territory almost always results in vicious fighting. The combatants lash out at each other with their feet and sharp spurs. Fights among gobblers often end in a death.

During breeding season, which is late winter or early spring, gobblers become even more ill-tempered. They display their feathers and will attack at the slightest provocation from another gobbler.

Turkey tail feather shown actual size.

The Merriam's turkey, a western subspecies, has distinctive white tips on its tail and on the feathers covering its tail.

When a gobbler displays its tail feathers, its head colors deepen. Its wattles swell, and its caruncle lengthens.

The hen turkey makes her nest in a quiet, secluded, secret place. There, in a shallow depression beside a boulder or at the base of a tree, she lays eight to eighteen large eggs. The eggs are tan and speckled brown to blend with the leaves and stones on the ground.

Turkey egg shown actual size.

A month after they are laid, the eggs hatch.

Baby turkeys are called poults. Very soon after they hatch, turkey poults are out of the nest and in the nearby grasses catching protein-rich insects they need for rapid growth.

The faster they grow the better off they are, in a world full of animals that like to eat turkeys. Turkey poults are killed by hungry foxes, coyotes, skunks, and owls.

As they grow bigger and stronger, young turkeys are less vulnerable to attack from small predators. A full grown turkey weighing fifteen to seventeen pounds is a powerful bird. It takes a coyote, wolf, bobcat, mountain lion, or human hunter to kill one.

Turkeys tend to run from danger, bursting into flight as a last resort.

A turkey's wings are built for short bursts of flight rather than long distance flying. Even so, turkeys can cover a lot of distance in the air. A flock of turkeys may alternate between feeding areas that are miles apart. The birds fly from one feeding spot to another.

Turkeys can fly fast—up to fifty miles per hour! They can fly high, clearing the tops of eighty-foot-tall trees, but most of their flight is low over fields, between tree trunks, or up to the branches of their "roost" tree—the tree where they spend the night.

Turkeys are not winter migrators. They stay in the same general area all year long, sleeping in the same trees night after night, high and safe from most predators. Some roost trees are small, with limbs enough for only a half dozen turkeys. Other roost trees are large enough for a whole flock.

Turkeys are survivors. Even in places where deep winter snow covers the ground seven months of the year, resident flocks of turkeys make it through. Today the wild turkey can be found in the north, south, east, and west. After so many years of decline, the wild turkey is seen by more people, in more places, than ever before.

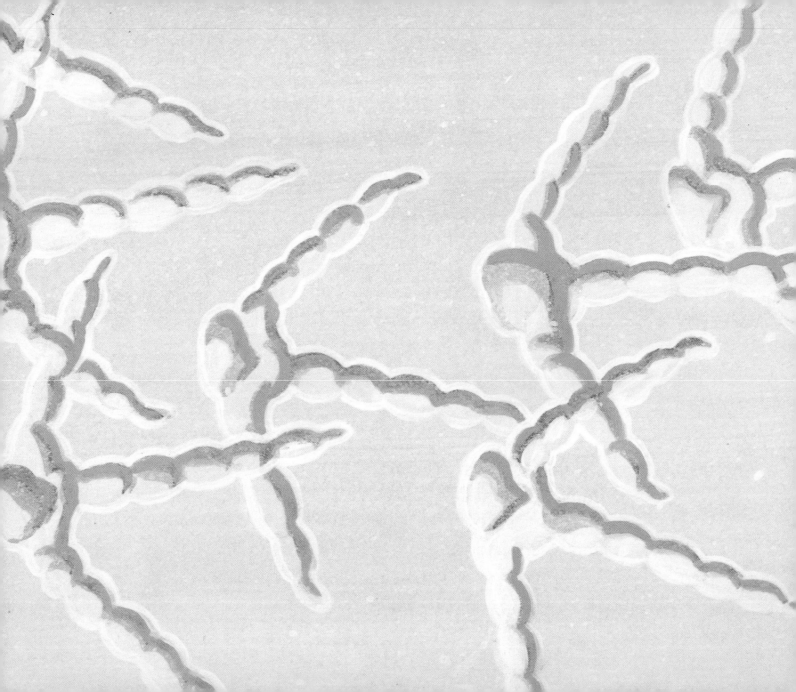

Michelle Sherburne

MEET JIM ARNOSKY

Jim Arnosky is the author and illustrator of nearly 100 books about wildlife and nature for children. He has received numerous honors for his work, including the American Association for the Advancement of Science Lifetime Achievement Award for excellence in science illustration.

For this book, Jim drew on years of careful observation of wild turkeys in his home state of Vermont and other parts of the country. His vibrant, detailed illustrations are based on his own photography and video taken in the wild.

When he is not traveling to visit schools and explore nature, Jim Arnosky lives in Vermont, with his wife, Deanna.